CADAQUÉS

CADAQUÉS

PHOTOGRAPHY Jordi Puig | TEXT Cristina Masanés

TRIANGLE ▼ POSTALS

Cadaqués, with its remarkable character, leaves nobody indifferent to it. Everything is quite unique in this marine landscape. The quality of the light, the geological relief, the intensity of the blue, the care taken with the urban growth, the character of its inhabitants and its legendary past. Nevertheless, nothing would be as it is without a decisive factor: the geographical isolation. Even today access is not easy and one hundred years ago reaching Cadaqués was a journey worthy of Ulysses.

Was this what the people who arrived at the village at the turn of the century were looking for? Probably. Cadaqués was discovered by writers and painters in the 20s and by the travelling bohemia of the 60s. Salvador Dalí, who loved this village obsessively, contributed to its international projection. Since then, the streets of the village, the silence of its coves, the magic of the small bay of Portlligat and the rebellious geography of Cap de Creus (the cape of crosses) have made Cadaqués a trademark for the best Mediterranean tourism.

CONTENTS

A LEGENDARY PAST

A past of pirates and shipwrecks, of painters and coral hunters, of witches and fishermen. A legendary past. A unique
past for a unique village. The history of Cadaqués is inevitably
marked by its maritime condition and geographical isolation.
In Cadaqués, until just a few decades ago, everything came
and went by sea.

The origin of the village is as uncertain as that of its
name. Although no trace has ever been found to prove it, it is
said that the Greeks raised a temple devoted to Aphrodite in
some spot of Cap de Creus. The fact is that the first recorded
historical date goes back to the beginning of the 11th century,
when the village was a tiny sea port ascribed to –like a large
part of the Empordà lands– the domain of the monks of the
monastery of Sant Pere de Rodes and of the counts of Empú-
ries. We know that in the 13th century, the small seafaring
community was governed by a singular –and unique in the
area– system of direct democracy: the general meetings of residents were held in the church square to decide on the mat-
ters affecting the community. When, in 1403, the king ordered that the village be governed by 12 illustrious men to be
chosen by the village, its inhabitants complained. Even then
Cadaqués displayed its own personality.

We must imagine medieval Cadaqués as a small walled
precinct raised on a rocky hill alongside the sea. One of the old
gateways that leads to the old centre is still conserved, the Portal d'Avall or Portal del Mar. Close to the sea a semi-cylindrical
tower is also conserved –where the actual town hall is housed–
that rests over some rocks intermittently beaten by the sea's
waves. It is the Punta des Baluard, a defence tower that was in-
dispensable when Cadaqués only possessed the wits of its inhabitants and the uncertain luck that came from the sea. The
reason for this is that in the 14th, 15th and 16th centuries the
Mediterranean was in no way whatsoever the safe place it is
today.

In 1444, twenty-two Moorish galleons burnt down the village. One hundred years later, it was the Turkish pirate known as Redbeard who, with twenty-five boats, looted the village and burnt down the church. Over and over again Genovese corsairs and Algerian pirates attacked a people who lived in a remote corner of the world. The constant battles of the country with the French neighbours –there was more than one invasion by the French army– were added to this past which, seen through contemporary eyes, takes on a legendary status. The village archives contain the documental evidence that backs up its true history.

During the 18th century piracy decreased in the Mediterranean. Trade with America was liberalised, a circumstance that stimulated overseas navigation. In Cadaqués vine cultivation was intensified. The outskirts of the village filled with paths and hillside terraces of vineyards skilfully built with dry stone by the locals. The rough land of Cap de Creus was transformed into a veritable garden of vines. 1800 marked the age of splendour for the village in terms of seafaring. Huge ships set sail from the small port of Cadaqués with destinations to Cuba, Italy and France. They carried wine and strong spirits, products that were highly valued by international trade. Everybody worked: the barrel makers manufactured equipment for the wine and the salting factories provided employment for the women of the village. The ships transported highly valued cargo such as tobacco and smuggling activities increased. The red coral of the area, of a unique quality, attracted coral hunters from distant lands. They were the prosperous years and the village extended its frontiers beyond the old centre. Notable eighteenth-century buildings such as the Casino bear witness to those years. In 1883 the phylloxera pest that came from France and affected the vines reached Cadaqués. It was the end of the vine. The end of trade. The end of a century.

As a result of the phylloxera crisis, the people of Cadaqués emigrated to distant lands, above all to Cuba. Some of them, in time, returned as rich men to show off their fortunes with modernist houses that are still standing today. They were the *Americanos,* the ones who had got rich in the Americas. Others returned with their pockets empty. When in Cadaqués it was said of somebody, "that one's suitcase has fallen into the water," everyone knew that he had been unlucky. Those that stayed behind suffered the poverty of the early decades of the 20th century and the uncertainty of a civil war.

20th century Cadaqués very soon met its first visitors. They came from the city and knew how to see the unique possibilities provided by this seafaring spot. After them, it was Salvador Dalí who opened up Cadaqués to the world. With him arrived sixty aristocrats, artists, show business celebrities and travelling souls in search of something only Cadaqués could provide them with: a retreat with freedom close to the sea. Since then, tourism has grown year after year, compensated however, by a sensible level of urban development.

CADAQUÉS

Situated in the easternmost point of the Costa Brava, the district of Cadaqués is the first within the Iberian Peninsula to see the sun rise in the morning. Two hills surround the Cadaqués area and contribute to its isolation. To the north, towards Port de la Selva, is Puig de Bufadors and to the south, towards Roses, the Pení mountain, at 613 metres altitude and of a singular outline. *Pennos* is a Celtic word that means "nearly the end". In the Empordà county they used to say that after the Pení there was nothing else, just the sea. Even today, the access by road gives an idea of the level of age-old isolation that the village has experienced: facing the sea and with its back to the land. The road was not built until the beginning of the 20th century. It is no coincidence that they say that the sailors knew the distant ports before they knew Barcelona, three days journey away. It is also the case that, when the sea took the men away for days on end, a matriarchal system was established in the village. It is no surprise that Cadaqués still preserves its own special way of speaking: known as *salat,* with the *la* article being replaced by *sa,* a particular trait shared with other points of the Mediterranean such as the Balearic Isles.

When we cross the Perafita pass and begin to descend, the white relief of the village against the blue background hints at a kind of promise. During the journey, the landscape displays its peculiar geological constitution. It is a country made of lead grey and very harsh greens: slate and olive greens and an excessive light. A country untiringly fanned by the *Tramontana* wind, a dry and cold wind that comes from the north and produces a strange luminosity. An abrupt land that was ordered by patient hands into terraces and dry stone walls.

Cadaqués, however, is nothing without the sea. Once having reached the village, and facing the bay, you realise that you find yourself in a world outside the world. The village spreads across to one of the deepest and most sheltered bays on the Costa Brava. Towards the south, until Cala Nans. Towards the north, to the island of S'Arenella and the characteristic crag of Es Cucurucuc. To the right and left, a strip of seafront opens out that combines small coves and beaches with the white of the houses and streets. This is the bay of Cadaqués, populated by a mosaic of boats that turn it into one of the liveliest bays in the region.

The layout of the village is the best record of its past. The old centre, once walled, is raised on a hill to the side of the stream. It preserves the portal facing the sea –the one that closed off the village higher up has disappeared– along with the silence of its steep and narrow streets. At the top of the hill is the church of Santa María, of a singular presence and one of the most painted of the Costa Brava. Dalí, Magritte and Picasso were some of its interpreters.

When the old church was burnt down by Turkish pirates, it was decided to build a new church with the money from the fishermen who had gone to sea on forbidden days, when a religious festival had to be held. The accounts were tallied once a year and thanks to the fines work was started on the building which today determines the village's profile. In 1641 the central aisle and facade were officially opened, although the whole work was not completed until the end of the 18th century. The sculptor from Vic, Pau Costa, among others, was chosen to produce one of the scenographic Baroque altarpieces, with more life and movement... the most notable of those that have survived in the Empordà. The church walls have experienced the privilege of hearing the leading voices and notes of the International Music Festival that since the seventies has been held every summer in Cadaqués. Jean-Pierre Rampal, Montserrat Caballé, Victoria de los Ángeles... The cypress trees at the entrance, the semicircular arch doorway, the bell-cote, and the church tower welcomes us to a unique view over the rooftops and the bay.

From one side to the other of the old centre the village grew in the years of trade and vineyards. Diverse buildings bear witness to this. Among them, the Casino, a nineteenth-century building situated just at the end of the Platja Llarga beach, beside the stream. Over one hundred years ago, the village's heart beat in the café on the ground floor. Restored with good taste, the first two floors provide an excellent venue for exhibitions. The Casa Serinyana, known as the *casa blaua* (the blue house) due to the shade of its facade tiling, is a turn-of-the-century modernist house. The plant shapes of the windows and wrought iron work of the balconies are modernist. Further on, in Riba des Pianc, Casa Colom, today empty but showing signs of a glorious past.

Among the list of visitors, Cadaqués has been the port of call of famous architects. Some of them, such as Lanfranco Bombelli, J. A. Coderch and O. Tusquets contributed actively to the remodelling of the village, necessary to make room for the tourism, but undertaken with the respect that other towns on the Costa Brava have not enjoyed. Today, a strict ruling requires all buildings to be low in height, thus preserving the autochthonous architecture.

Cadaqués, nevertheless, has for many years been a veritable republic of the arts. The Pitxot family, a saga of musicians and painters, were the pioneers of tourism in the village at the beginning of the century. The family house, Des Sortell, in the far south of the village, played host to the first visitors: Pablo Picasso, René Magritte, Isaac Albéniz or Santiago Rusiñol were some of them. In the thirties, Salvador Dalí, who had spent his summers in Cadaqués since he had been a boy, turned it into his home and playing host to a notable guest list: Luis Buñuel, Federico García Lorca, André Breton, Paul Eluard, René Crevel and Marcel Duchamp were just the first ones. As years went by, the name of Cadaqués attracted painters, intellectuals, bohemians and an eccentricity loving *gauche divine*. In the sixties and seventies, the Hostal in the main passage, an *indiana* house, owned by a returning émigré who had made good in Cuba, and decorated and run by Pierre Lottier, provided the most magical nights. Nights of good jazz and surreal perfume where Dalí strolled by now and again. The Hostal, the Cafè de l'Havana, the Frontera, the Marítim, the Boia, the Melitón... were the bars and cafés that witnessed the conversations and arguments in all languages. Numerous art galleries and painters' studios opened up. Cadaqués had become universal.

Some time ago, to the south of Cap de Creus, a village changed fishing and vineyards for tourism and art. With a surprisingly cosmopolitan willingness, it was able to conserve what other spots lose more easily, its identity. An exceptional retreat of light where everything, or nearly everything, is possible.

"Cadaqués, this is the place I have adored all my life with a fanatical loyalty". Already in his early paintings, such as this *Port Alguer* from 1924, a very young Dalí reproduced one of the most loved spots of Cadaqués, Portdoguer –previously Portalguer– and the Riba Pitxot.

A landmark for tourists and fishermen alike, the church of Santa María, at the highest point of the old centre, identifies the village's profile. Built with fishermen's money in the 16th and 17th centuries, it houses an exuberant polychromed altarpiece with an impeccable scenography and quite unique in the Empordà county.

Old Cadaqués

Blue, green and red on white. This is the chromatic palette of old Cadaqués, a network of steep and narrow lanes, which patient hands paved with slate slabs and pebbles from the sea in a unique local style that is known as *rastell* (spiked or raked paving, coming from the Roman *opus spicatum*). The houses, carefully restored, bear witness to a poor past. You can still see the odd bread oven, which, like a vestige, sticks out from the old facades. Conserving instead of demolishing is part of the singularity of a village that has shown remarkable sensitivity towards its autochthonous architecture.

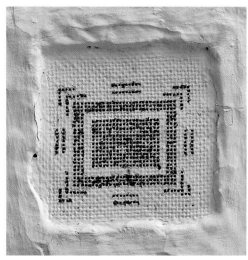

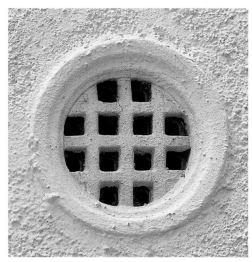

Pirates and corsairs

The old quarter reminds us of dangers that come from the sea when you least expect them. Closed within a wall, it could be entered by different gateways. The Portal d'Avall, facing the beach, is the only one that is preserved. It is a covered passage between two arches that was once closed with a wooden door. Further down, a defence tower is preserved that, before the construction of the Riba, was erected over the rocks: it is the Punta des Baluard, where the Town Hall is today. El Call street, which goes round it, bears witness to the old Jewish quarter. The church of Santa María crowns the old quarter, an area rich in silence and voices from the past.

"Whoever tries Cadaqués never forgets it". The writer Josep Pla, one who has written about this seaside village best, knew of its effects very well when one arrives for the very first time and finds it very difficult to leave.

La Rambla or Passeig, the village's nerve centre,
extends parallel to the Platja Llarga beach. Standing
out, at the end, is the fine building of the Casino.
In its café, behind large windows bathed in light, the
heart of the village has beat for many years. Its upper
floors, recently restored with great care, house a large
space for exhibitions and art shows.

The Casa Colom, the *blaua* (blue) house or Casa
Serinyana, the Casino... the nineteenth-century and
modernist buildings that we find along the village
seafront tells us of a time of prosperity, when the vineyards and overseas navigation made the modest economy of a seafaring village grow. Some of those that went
to America returned wealthy and built richly decorated
generous buildings.

A bay open to blue

Cadaqués is, nevertheless, as well as its white streets, an immense bay open to the sea. The Passeig and the Platja Llarga have always played host to, in winter and summer, visitors and fishermen who for centuries dried their fishing nets and repaired their fishing boats. Today it is the liveliest cafés where the conversations and reading take place. Opposite them, a mosaic made of boats fills the bay. In the background, the rock of Es Cucurucuc, with a peculiar name and outline, observes village life from a distance. Some say it owes its name to its pyramidal shape or of a *cucurucho,* or cone. Salvador Dalí looks at us elegantly to remind us that, before us, he had already said that this was the most beautiful village in the world.

Cadaqués and its light possess the strange ability of stopping time.

They say that in Cadaqués they have always loved coffee. The women made it in huge saucepans. Today, the village has a big choice of cafés and terraces. The Marítimo bar was the first: even in the thirties the fishermen gathered there and discussed the state of the sea and life in the village. The Boia, beside it, replaced a huge buoy that, when the sea was rough, warned the boats with a characteristic sound.

The quality of the water and the rocky landscape of an
irregular coastline have always been one of the Costa
Brava's great assets. The beaches and coves of
Cadaqués tempt you to swim in them.

Festivals all year round

The carnival in February, with its popular *garotada* (sea urchin meal), is a chance to give rein to all the characters of popular imagination. Carnival is experienced with great intensity for a few days in Cadaqués. In summer, the most important festival is that of the Virgin of Carmen, with its regattas of boats and its lateen sail races. It is also in summer when the International Music Festival, a pioneer event on the Costa Brava more than thirty years ago, has brought world famous musicians and singers to the village. Every summer there is an interesting programme. In winter, it is the turn of the annual pilgrimage of Sant Sebastià, in the hermitage of the same name, bringing together the locals in a festival where they dance *patacades*, a dance accompanied by ironic lyrics regarding village life. Finally, at the first light of New Year, on the 1st of January, a celebration is held in the Cap de Creus lighthouse with *sardana* dancing and chocolate.

From the sea to the stove

Cadaqués' gastronomic repertoire ranks amongst the best to be found along the coast. In different settings, there is enough on offer to cover all tastes and all budgets. Since the fish caught varies throughout the year, it is best to order the fresh fish of the day. Sardine, horse mackerel, Atlantic mackerel... aromas from the sea and essential flavours. The list is very long indeed but if you want two exquisite classics, try the *suquet* (a typical fish stew) and the baked sea bass. The sea urchins, the *garotes,* are caught in autumn and winter. The rock mussels from the Cap de Creus coves are not easily forgotten. And for dessert, sweets. The *taps* from Cadaqués –in the photo– conveniently flambéed with rum, could be a delicious farewell to a delicious meal.

Witches and spells

It is said that in Cadaqués, as in other isolated spots close to the sea, when the fishing and seafaring took the men away for days at a time, in the village a republic was established of the womenfolk in which they practiced witchcraft. Xumeua, Patum... were they witches as has been said? What is true is that the women played a vital role in village life. Their names and nicknames have often been used as the family surname or the names of the houses. They carried pitchers around the streets on their heads in an image reproduced by different painters and illustrators which today can be seen as an icon of the Cadaqués of yesteryear. On the beach, the boats and their names are the small homage to the wives of the men who still live off the sea.

The flat beach of Es Llané, at the extreme south of the village, received the first summer visitors and it was here where they built the first houses. Amongst them, that of the of the notary Salvador Dalí, father of the painter, who in the twenties put up figures such as Federico García Lorca and Luis Buñuel. At the end of Es Llané, if you follow the path, you leave behind the Es Sortell peninsula and reach the Cala Nans lighthouse, which closes the bay of Cadaqués.

ROUTE 1 **MYTHICAL CADAQUÉS**

If it is true, as they say, that time does not pass in Cadaqués, then it will be easy for us to do a tour of the settings painted, written about and experienced by the artists who, from the beginning of the 20th century, took refuge in this village and who have formed the more mythical Cadaqués.

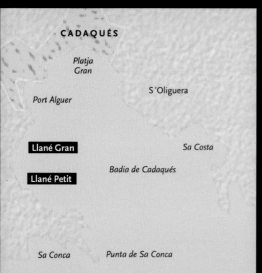

CADAQUÉS

Platja Gran

S´Oliguera

Port Alguer

Llané Gran

Sa Costa

Badia de Cadaqués

Llané Petit

Sa Conca   Punta de Sa Conca

Recitals and Scripts. The beach of Es LLané, in the southernmost end of the town, was the spot where, in January 1930, Salvador Dalí and Luis Buñuel were preparing the script for the surrealist film *L'Âge d'or*. A few months later the outdoor scenes of the film were shot in Cap de Creus. Max Ernst played a bandit and one of the voiceover's was that of Paul Eluard. Some years before, in 1925 and 1927, Es Llane had played host to the poetry readings and recitals of Federico García Lorca before the Dalí family. Lorca was a passionate admirer of the village.

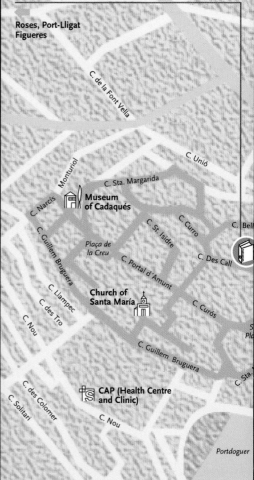

Written-about corners. The writer Josep Pla spent many seasons in Cadaqués. In the end, he bought a house in the Es Call street. In love with this landscape and with great descriptive skill, his tales are the best portrait of the village. Before the afternoon nap, you could find him chatting in the cafés of the Passeig with his pipe tobacco. He could be identified by his beret.

Roses, Port-Lligat
Figueres

C. de la Font Vella

C. Unió

C. Sta. Margarida

Monturiol

C. Narcís

Museum of Cadaqués

C. Curro

C. Bell

C. St. Isidre

C. Guillem Bruguera

Plaça de la Creu

C. Des Call

C. Portal d´Amunt

C. Llampec

C. des Tro

Church of Santa María

C. Curós

C. Nou

C. Guillem Bruguera

C. Sta.

Pla

C. des Colomer

CAP (Health Centre and Clinic)

C. Solitari

C. Nou

Portdoguer

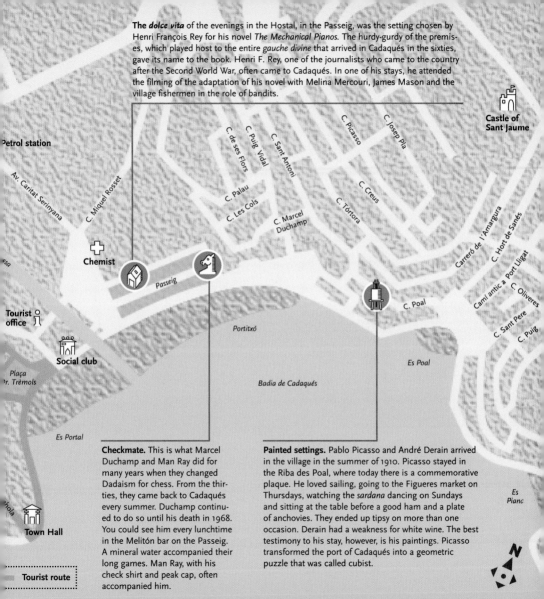

The *dolce vita* of the evenings in the Hostal, in the Passeig, was the setting chosen by Henri François Rey for his novel *The Mechanical Pianos*. The hurdy-gurdy of the premises, which played host to the entire *gauche divine* that arrived in Cadaqués in the sixties, gave its name to the book. Henri F. Rey, one of the journalists who came to the country after the Second World War, often came to Cadaqués. In one of his stays, he attended the filming of the adaptation of his novel with Melina Mercouri, James Mason and the village fishermen in the role of bandits.

Castle of Sant Jaume

Petrol station

Av. Caritat Serinyana

C. Miquel Rosset

C. de ses Flors

C. Puig Vidal

C. Sant Antoni

C. Palau

C. Les Cols

C. Picasso

C. Josep Pla

C. Creus

C. Tòrtora

C. Marcel Duchamp

Carreró de l'Amargura

C. Hort de Sanés

Camí antic a Port Lligat

C. Oliveres

C. Sant Pere

C. Puig

Chemist

Passeig

C. Poal

Tourist office

Portitxó

Es Poal

Social club

Plaça Dr. Trèmols

Badia de Cadaqués

Es Portal

Es Pianc

Town Hall

Checkmate. This is what Marcel Duchamp and Man Ray did for many years when they changed Dadaism for chess. From the thirties, they came back to Cadaqués every summer. Duchamp continued to do so until his death in 1968. You could see him every lunchtime in the Melitón bar on the Passeig. A mineral water accompanied their long games. Man Ray, with his check shirt and peak cap, often accompanied him.

Painted settings. Pablo Picasso and André Derain arrived in the village in the summer of 1910. Picasso stayed in the Riba des Poal, where today there is a commemorative plaque. He loved sailing, going to the Figueres market on Thursdays, watching the *sardana* dancing on Sundays and sitting at the table before a good ham and a plate of anchovies. They ended up tipsy on more than one occasion. Derain had a weakness for white wine. The best testimony to his stay, however, is his paintings. Picasso transformed the port of Cadaqués into a geometric puzzle that was called cubist.

.... Tourist route

PORTLLIGAT

We will never know what would have been the fate of the small bay of Portlligat if Salvador Dalí had not converted it into his place in the world. What is true is that, even before him, for the fishermen of Cadaqués, this bay closed by two isles that protect it from the open sea, was one of the most appreciated corners in the district. Dalí turned it into a universally projected landscape. He had a sharp eye in his choice, a very sharp eye indeed.

Situated to the north of the village of Cadaqués, the bay of Portlligat forms a natural port of calm waters and exceptional light surrounded by the isle of Portlligat and by the tiny isle of Sa Farnera. Since 1953, at the behest of and with the involvement of Salvador Dalí, a foundation protects the bay from the property development whirlpool. On the land, it is surrounded by olive groves in an atavistic and sober landscape that heralds an advance notice of what begins a little further north: the mineral geology of Cap de Creus. From the sea, its almost circular land relief turns it into a typical bay. As the writer Josep Pla said, "it is, in fact, one of the coves on the coast that creates the illusion of living in the pure intimacy of the sea". This is what the fishermen found when they anchored in search of a calm shelter. This is what Salvador Dalí was able to see, knowing the spot well from his family boat trips when he had been a boy. This is what one still experiences today when facing the bay.

The isle of Portlligat or the isle of Correu (Post Office) –the village postman lived on it for many years–, half a kilometre long and in the shape of a dragon, is an isle with little vegetation –scrubland and bushes– where decades before there had been houses inhabited by people from the village. Later on, by the seventies, a hippy colony set up home on it spontaneously every summer. Today, all the buildings have been demolished and it is uninhabited. Since 1989, the Special Protection Plan for the isle of Portlligat conserves it. This is, nonetheless, above all else a profile that identifies the bay.

Reproduced untiringly by the skilful hand of Salvador Dalí, it today forms part of the collective memory. It does not matter if we do not know Portlligat; on arriving, its relief of the sea enveloped by land and its calm waters are familiar to us, surprisingly familiar. As is its light. A light, in the eyes of Dalí, "one hundred years old, poor, serene and intrepid like the concise forehead of Minerva".

At the back of the bay is the hamlet of Portlligat, the old fishermen's refuge which was many years ago turned into a summer retreat and overlooked by Salvador Dalí's house. It is a hamlet as old as the village of Cadaqués, where the fishermen anchored when there had been a swell. Some of them ended up building a hut to keep their fishing tackle and spend the night. For them, the small beach of Portlligat was the spot for drying the nets, in other words, the clothesline. The hundred-year-old fishermen's huts are the origin of the Portlligat that we know today. They preserve their minimal architecture of elemental material and chimneys finished in a pyramid to protect the fire from the *Tramontana* wind. Today, as well as the old fishermen's houses converted into second homes, in Portlligat there is an unusual element that now forms part of the landscape: Salvador Dalí's house, which emerges in cube-shaped blocks and surreal suggestions. This building, along with the Theatre-Museum of Figueres and the Castle of Púbol, is one of the three essential spaces for anyone who wishes to approach and understand Dalí's universe.

This was the only permanent residence throughout the painter's long life. Here Dalí lived, painted, loved and invited figures from all over the world. From 1930 and almost until his death, Portlligat was a vital basic pictorial landscape. When Dalí bought the first fishermen's hut in 1930, it had absolutely nothing: no electricity or running water: nothing at all. Portlligat was a spot far away from everything, a spot to love Gala... and to paint. At night he worked with *petromax,* a lantern fuel used on the boats that fished by oil lamp. As the years passed by, he bought up different huts –eight in all– to form the whole building that we know today. Every autumn, "when the money ran out", Dalí and Gala changed the rocky silence of Portlligat for the hustle and bustle of Paris or New York. In spring they left the city, "like one leaves the pot full of tripe", and returned to the womb-like refuge of Portlligat. A refuge that was, for many years, a silent retreat: finally, however, in the seventies and eighties, the coaches arrived at Portlligat to see the painter, if only for a fleeting moment, in the garden. In 1997, eight years after the painter's death, the house was opened to the public.

Portlligat also has, apart from the central hamlet, a series of beaches and tiny coves. Southwards, following the shoreline where the fishermen dock, one reaches the long Cala Calders and the Ses Boquelles crossing, the closest point between the coast and the isle of Correu. In the opposite direction, towards the north, is an asphalted path that goes from the Platja de Portlligat to the cove of Sant Antoni. We can continue further on: a path close to the sea will lead us to the Cap de Creus lighthouse along silent coves: Jonquet, Guillola, Cala Bona and Jugadora. The greyish green of the olive groves reaches down as far as the water on an unforgettable route along the most mineral part of the Costa Brava.

To get to Portlligat, one can take the coastal path that, from Cadaqués, passes by the Es Caials beach, an important diving and underwater archaeology centre. If you prefer the inland route, by car or on foot, we will pass by the small hermitage of Sant Baldiri. A path leaves from the hermitage by which the fishermen reached a viewpoint to see what the weather was like and the state of the wind at Cap de Creus. Close to the hermitage is the cemetery of Cadaqués, one of the most beautiful on the Costa Brava. An easy-to- follow centenary route: a stroll that is well worth the effort.

On land, Portlligat is surrounded by olive groves and small coves, such as the Sant Antoni cove in the extreme north of the bay. From the sea, it is bordered by the isle of Portlligat or Correu, with an elongated outline, and by the tiny isle of Sa Farnera.

All the blues of Portlligat

"One of the driest, most mineral and planetary spots on the earth. The mornings provide wild and bitter joy [...]; the dusks are often morbidly sad, [...] in the evening, [...] the water is so still that it reflects the dramas of the twilight sky". It was Salvador Dalí who knew and painted each and every one of the blues of Portlligat. In winter, in summer, by day and by night. By his hand, this forgotten cove became a spot recognised all over the world. A spot which, despite receiving many visitors, still preserves the shades and luminous colours that captivated the painter's brush and glance.

Boats and fishermen

The fishermen of Cadaqués thought that Portlligat was a good shelter for boats. Today, tourism has been responsible for displacing the fishing activity but the locals, throughout their seafaring past, had developed their own methods such as oil lamp or net fishing. For oil lamp fishing they needed a large sailboat that transported the nets and several boats that would burn the lamps that attracted the fish in the darkness of the night. The art lay in casting a giant net out to sea. Once full, the fishermen, in two or more groups of five or six, pulled with all their strength towards land until they managed to hoist it and land it on the beach or on the rocks. The work of emptying the nets often turned into a big festival.

A unique house

It is difficult to imagine the beach at Portlligat without Salvador Dalí's house. Built from the fishermen's huts –Dalí bought the first in 1930–, the painter wanted the roofs to form a staggered landscape that dropped down to the sea. The master of works produced his desire most accurately. The result, a series of cubic blocks that maintain the simplicity of the original huts and where enormous plaster eggs stand out from the roof as well as the melancholic heads of Castor and Pollux. The autochthonous materials (lime, slate and esparto) were used wisely. On the exterior, in front of the first hut, Dalí placed the hundred-year-old cypress trees and his unique boat-cypress that invites us to visit a unique building. Now all we have to do is go through the door.

An enormous bear will have welcomed us in. We get to the different rooms in the house by going from one level to another rather than passing through a door, thus reflecting the original layout of the different original huts. The dining room and library represent a first sip of sobriety in the house enriched only by the elements of a really personal universe.

The patient work of the painter

Here, in the studio, behind some large windows with a magnificent view, Dalí produced some of his best paintings. Working with patience and leading a spartan life, he painted sitting on a small bulrush stool. As well as the classical easel, he built a metallic framework that he operated to move up and down the bigger format canvases, and which enabled him to work at the correct height. In the workshop of optical objects –reached by one of the stairways that form part of the universe of the House-Museum– all the painter's details and objects are preserved, both those of his painting side and his work as an alchemist and experimentalist.

In winter, Paris and New York. When Gala and Dalí
returned to Portlligat in summer, from their private life
only the photos that Gala decorated the dressing room
with remain. After the bedrooms and the dressing
room, the oval room awaits us, Gala's secret hideaway.

And outside... the garden: a garden made in white and olive greens that gradually dares to incorporate all the outrageous style and transgressions of *kitsch*. You just need to look at the swimming pool area to see how.

ROUTE 2 **A HUNDRED-YEAR-OLD PATH**

When Dalí settled in Portlligat he had to carry everything on the back of an ass. The journey from Cadaqués to Portlligat was a poor path walked by women and fishermen with large baskets of fish, olives and grapes. Nothing remains today of that solitary path. Nonetheless, the hundred-year-old olive trees, the calm water in the coves and the serene beauty of Portlligat have all been saved from the passing of time. Even today we can go for a stroll that in a short while will lead us to one of the internationally renowned corners of Cadaqués.

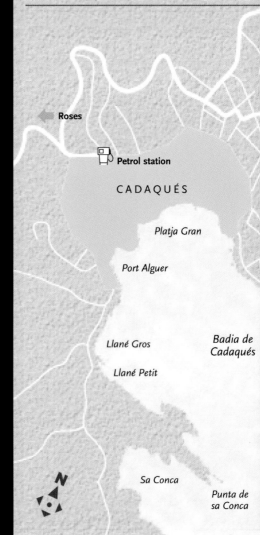

Hermitage of Sant Baldiri. If taking the inland route, the small hermitage of Sant Baldiri marks our path. It is a tiny Baroque building with a single nave and a portico with a segmented arch on the facade.

Roses

Petrol station

CADAQUÉS

Platja Gran

Port Alguer

Llané Gros

Badia de Cadaqués

Llané Petit

Sa Conca

Punta de sa Conca

N

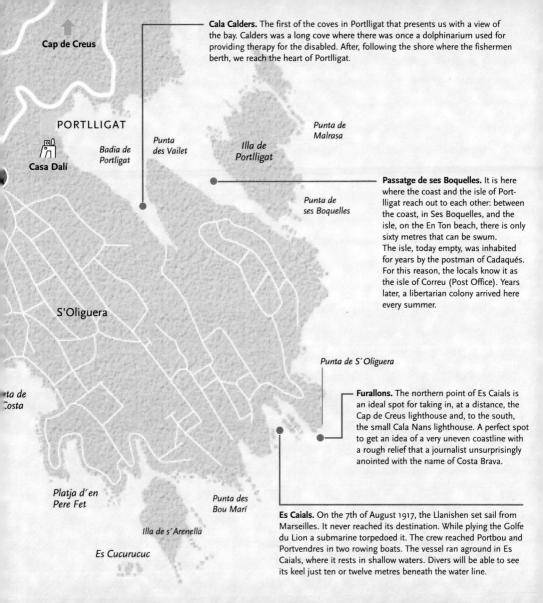

Cap de Creus

PORTLLIGAT

Casa Dalí

Badia de Portligat

Punta des Vailet

Illa de Portlligat

Punta de Malrasa

Punta de ses Boquelles

S'Oliguera

Punta de S´Oliguera

...ta de ...osta

Platja d´en Pere Fet

Punta des Bou Marí

Illa de s´Arenella

Es Cucurucuc

Cala Calders. The first of the coves in Portlligat that presents us with a view of the bay. Calders was a long cove where there was once a dolphinarium used for providing therapy for the disabled. After, following the shore where the fishermen berth, we reach the heart of Portlligat.

Passatge de ses Boquelles. It is here where the coast and the isle of Portlligat reach out to each other: between the coast, in Ses Boquelles, and the isle, on the En Ton beach, there is only sixty metres that can be swum.
The isle, today empty, was inhabited for years by the postman of Cadaqués. For this reason, the locals know it as the isle of Correu (Post Office). Years later, a libertarian colony arrived here every summer.

Furallons. The northern point of Es Caials is an ideal spot for taking in, at a distance, the Cap de Creus lighthouse and, to the south, the small Cala Nans lighthouse. A perfect spot to get an idea of a very uneven coastline with a rough relief that a journalist unsurprisingly anointed with the name of Costa Brava.

Es Caials. On the 7th of August 1917, the Llanishen set sail from Marseilles. It never reached its destination. While plying the Golfe du Lion a submarine torpedoed it. The crew reached Portbou and Portvendres in two rowing boats. The vessel ran aground in Es Caials, where it rests in shallow waters. Divers will be able to see its keel just ten or twelve metres beneath the water line.

CAP DE CREUS

I t is said that in ancient times they erected a temple in honour of Aphrodite on this cape. No remains have ever been found of it but in Roman chronicles the place is known as cape *Aphrodisium*. For seafarers it has always been the cape of the Devil. For us, since medieval times, due to the hermitages, monasteries and crosses with which the district boundaries were marked on Christianisation of the area, it has been the Cap de Creus (crosses).

Cap de Creus is a peninsula that projects ten kilometres into the Mediterranean compared to the general line that the Costa Brava follows. From the air it has a branching effect with the appearance of a plane tree leaf. From land it is a mineral world of hard beauty and great geological interest. From the sea it is a very rugged coastline that contains some of the most difficult navigational points in the Mediterranean. It is a mountainous area of 9,900 hectares where the agitated Pyrenees reach the sea. Cap de Creus was declared a Natural Park in 1998 in order to protect it, the marine environs and the Verdera mountain range. Cala Tamariua, in the district of Port de la Selva, and Punta Falconera, in Roses, are the northern and southern borders respectively.

In medieval times the Cap de Creus peninsula was populated by vines and terraces, farms and flocks of sheep, flour mills and a multitude of dry stone huts that gave a rebellious landscape a human touch. Today it is empty. After the phylloxera pest at the end of the 19th century, and the later fires, Cap de Creus is a bare landscape exposed to the wind. The cattle, which spend summer in the high parts of the Pyrenees, graze here in winter as if they were a vestige of the ancient seasonal migration. The only other presence is that of the curious walkers and alert geologists who know its hidden corners.

Two elements make Cap de Creus a unique landscape; the effects of the *Tramontana,* the intense northerly wind, and the geological composition of its ground. The *Tramontana* has carved out an abrupt and dramatic relief and has determined its plantlife. The water from the torrents and streams have moulded a craggy landscape of deep ravines inhabited by thicket, scrubland and other bushes which, due to the mechanical effect of the wind, have taken on peculiar shapes. There are also junipers *(càdecs* in Catalan), a strange bush whose name, according to some theories, would be the origin of the name of Cadaqués. Cap de Creus, however, is an international place of interest due to its unique geology.

Pegmatite is a light rounded rock that rarely combines with schist in the way it does in Cap de Creus. Schist, in contrast, is dark and laminated; the water softens it patiently and the *Tramontana,* corrosive like the salt and sand it carries, chisels it as the years pass by. Through a striking process of metamorphism, with the passing of time the schist has become eroded and has formed the uneven rocks we can see today. They are angular rocks that have taken on a very particular morphology, above all on the coastal stretch and, specifically, on the so-called "golden kilometre of Cap de Creus": a solitary section on the northern side of the cape. It is the part that goes from Cala Culip to Pla de Tudela. There the landscape is made up exclusively of coagula of rock that change shape as you move past them. Here are rocks like zoomorphic sculptures, taking on the form that the observer gives them. In this way the rocks form eagles, lions, turtles... Dalí had no problem in inventing the figures of changing shapes in his paintings: he just had to open his eyes and look carefully... and of course, paint.

From Cadaqués, a road takes us to the eastern extreme of the cape. The best route, however, is the old path that leaves the village and runs along the sinuous edge of Cap de Creus to take us as far as the lighthouse and the old border guards' barracks. It was a windproof barracks built in 1914 as a strategic border post. There, overlooking the wide horizon of the Golfe du Lion, we can appreciate that this sea of dolphins hides a past of shipwrecks and that in its coves lies one of the important underwater archaeological finds in the Mediterranean. It is not the cliffs –more impressive on other parts of the coast– that turn this coastal area into a danger for the seafarer, but rather the brusqueness in the change of orientation. Before the lighthouse, which stands seventy five metres above the sea, the coastline turns sharply and faces the north. An extremely sharp turn that, for the sailors of Cadaqués, separates the *Mar d'Amunt,* the northern sea, from that of the south (*Mar d'Avall).* In the north the sea is open to the *Tramontana.* In the south, until reaching Cadaqués, the coast extends calmly. On the last part of the road, before reaching the lighthouse, a straight part enables us to observe the contrast: to the left, the beaten rocks of Culip, and to the right, the calm waters of Cala Jugadora.

The Cap de Creus lighthouse possesses all the ingredients for a good novel. Opened in 1853, on a spot occupied by a watch tower, the lighthouse sticks out into the sea and is one of the most punished lighthouses in the country: the wind can blow at 150 kph. In this no-man's land the lighthouse keepers soon applied for a transfer. Who remembers the windy nights of the old lighthouse keepers of Devil's cape? "The lighthouse has been keeping watch for 3,000 years and has experienced 700 shipwrecks. It has the look of the bottom of the sea and always cries out bad omens". This is the poet Miquel Desclot who, quietly, has guarded its memory.

All possible shapes

A landscape made of wind and rocks. The *Tramontana* and the salt have sculpted the rocks with holes and fanciful illustrations. Among its unique forms stands out the curious combination between blocks of light and dark rocks. Schist, a slaty and dark rock, has been mixed, over centuries, with the big white blocks of pegmatite. The strong fold in the land has registered dramatic folds and undulations. The result is a mineral landscape where the rocks have taken on the form randomly chosen by the elements. Zoomorphic rocks that change as you move past them: lions, eagles, camels... At first sight, Cap de Creus seems to contain absolutely nothing. But it only appears so, for if one knows how to look, this empty landscape contains all the shapes possible.

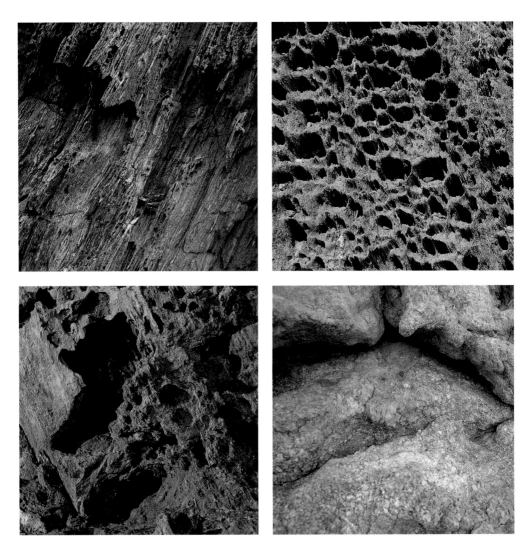

It is an area of marine mammals, above all dolphins, and the occasional whale that sporadically approaches the coastline. In deeper waters, one can see the coral reefs, a protected species that was once the main trade of this coast. The best red coral, called bull's blood, grows in the waters of Cap de Creus.

The Tramontana, "this inclement and tenacious land
wind that carries with it the seeds of madness", as well
as being worthy of a tale by Gabriel García Márquez,
has also created a crawling plant life of hemispherical
shapes. Junipers, heather, black rockrose, rosemary and
Balearic astragal all populate the surface of Cap de Creus.

El Mar d'Amunt (the north sea)

The Cap de Creus peninsula draws a sharp pointed form into the sea. It is on its northern side, in the Mar d'Amunt (north sea), where the scenery is more rugged and solitary, more windswept and rebellious. It is here where the Pyrenees reach the sea, as Dalí said, "in a grandiose geological delirium". From Cala Culip to Portaló it is an unpopulated setting inhabited only by mirages. This is the section of coastline that has experienced more shipwrecks and where the rescue work has always been more complicated. Like any good seafarer knows, negotiating the waters of the Mar d'Amunt on days with the northerly wind is a risky manoeuvre. For seafaring it has always been Devil's cape.

The section from Pla de Tudela to Cala Culip introduces us to the best rocky scenery. In Tudela, where in 1962 a French company built an irreverent holiday *ville,* are the Eagle and Camel, two of the cape's three starring rocks. The third, which was reproduced by Dalí in his painting *The Great Masturbator,* can be seen in the tiny Cala Culleró.

The nymph Calypso was a daughter of Atlas who, in love with Ulysses, held him prisoner for seven years. Her link with Culip is not clear, although it is known that it gets its name from her. It is a deep cove of sunken boats known for its underwater archaeological excavations.

Finisterrae

The extreme east of Cap de Creus, crowned by the lighthouse, separates the *Mar d'Amunt* from the *Mar d'Avall* (south sea). It is the point where the coastline and its waters draw a very sharp turn. To the south, the coastline extends calmly. Towards the north, it is open to the Tramontana wind. From the lighthouse you can make out the Golfe du Lion, so huge it fills up the entire sight. In front, the isle of Sa Rata or Massa d'Or, and further into the distance, to the north, the isle of S'Encalladora. The lighthouse, eternally beaten by the wind, was built in the mid-19th century on the spot where a watchtower had stood. Today, as well as being a spacious terrace for enjoying an aperitif, it houses the Espai Cap de Creus centre. Behind the lighthouse is the border guards' barracks built in 1914, a strategic point due to its closeness to the frontier from where smuggling was controlled. It is a windproof building with an arms room on the ground floor and the soldiers' quarters on the first floor. It is a restaurant with spectacular views and a strange atmosphere.

El Mar d'Avall (the south sea)

From the Cap de Creus lighthouse until Cadaqués extends the Mar d'Avall (the south sea). It is a calm sea sheltered from the *tramontana* on a very jagged coast where there is a succession of coves, caves, headlands and islets. Jugadora, Guillola, Jonquet... a coastline to spend, in the words of Pla, "eight days of summer, without newspapers or news, [...] where both dreams and the pots of fish in the stern of a boat sway". They say that every season in Cala Jugadora the fishermen played cards for the fishing sites. According to others, they played cards when they were sheltering from the bad weather and waiting for the calm to return. Whatever the case, it is a gentle cove and a good place to weigh anchor and with lovely scenery. In Cala Guillola, the weather and the fishing are usually unbeatable. As regards Cala Jonquet, the legend is that it was the regular landing point for smugglers.

ROUTE 3 **THE FIRST LIGHT OF DAY**

There where the Iberian Peninsula stretches out towards the east. There where the first light of day appears. There where Cap de Creus offers itself to the sea. This is a route along the easternmost end of Cap de Creus, an uninhabited landscape of rugged botany that shows us, live, the geological history of the planet. In the water it is a section that accumulates strong sea currents. From land, we are presented with a generous light and some quite unique views: a coastal route that leaves from the lighthouse and returns, an hour and a half later, to the point of departure.

Illa de Culleró

Sa Ferradura

Mar d´Amun

Furallons de Culi

Punta
Fe

Es Burro

Cala
Culip

S´Aragà

S´Arenella
de Culip

Roses, Cadaqués
Portlligat

Es Barrilers

N

Scenic points of interest

The end of the world. The path keeps close to the coastline going north until reaching the point where the so-called *The Lighthouse at the End of the World* was. It was a lighthouse erected in 1970 as a filming prop for the film *The Lighthouse at the End of the World* based on the novel of the same name by Jules Verne about the mythical lighthouse of Patagonia Argentina and starring Kirk Douglas and Yul Bryner. It was demolished in 1998. On the left, following the path, we reach Cala Culip. On the other side we can see some fishermen's huts. The same path takes us back to the lighthouse.

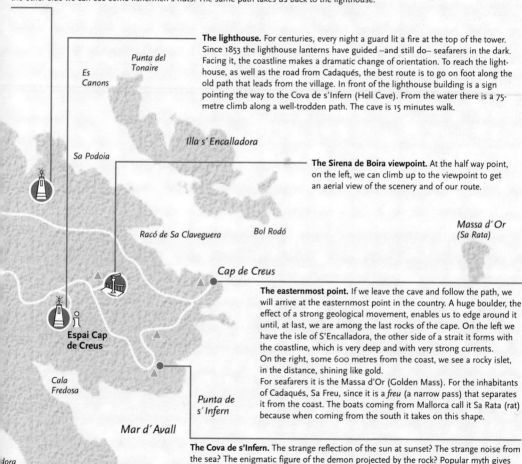

Punta del Tonaire

Es Canons

Illa s´Encalladora

Sa Podoia

The lighthouse. For centuries, every night a guard lit a fire at the top of the tower. Since 1853 the lighthouse lanterns have guided —and still do— seafarers in the dark. Facing it, the coastline makes a dramatic change of orientation. To reach the lighthouse, as well as the road from Cadaqués, the best route is to go on foot along the old path that leads from the village. In front of the lighthouse building is a sign pointing the way to the Cova de s'Infern (Hell Cave). From the water there is a 75-metre climb along a well-trodden path. The cave is 15 minutes walk.

The Sirena de Boira viewpoint. At the half way point, on the left, we can climb up to the viewpoint to get an aerial view of the scenery and of our route.

Racó de Sa Claveguera   *Bol Rodó*

Massa d´Or (Sa Rata)

Cap de Creus

Espai Cap de Creus

The easternmost point. If we leave the cave and follow the path, we will arrive at the easternmost point in the country. A huge boulder, the effect of a strong geological movement, enables us to edge around it until, at last, we are among the last rocks of the cape. On the left we have the isle of S'Encalladora, the other side of a strait it forms with the coastline, which is very deep and with very strong currents.
On the right, some 600 metres from the coast, we see a rocky islet, in the distance, shining like gold.
For seafarers it is the Massa d'Or (Golden Mass). For the inhabitants of Cadaqués, Sa Freu, since it is a *freu* (a narrow pass) that separates it from the coast. The boats coming from Mallorca call it Sa Rata (rat) because when coming from the south it takes on this shape.

Cala Fredosa

Punta de s´Infern

Mar d´Avall

dora

The Cova de s'Infern. The strange reflection of the sun at sunset? The strange noise from the sea? The enigmatic figure of the demon projected by the rock? Popular myth gives it a rich etymology. The fact is that water erosion has forged an enormous cavity in the rock that penetrates 100 metres into the mountain and makes it accessible in a medium-sized boat. Botany lovers will really enjoy the peculiar varieties of plants in the area.

Es Forcats

ALBUM OF CADAQUÉS

Without doubt, places would not be what they are without their people, with their way of life and way or ordering the world. Even more so in Cadaqués, where the geographical isolation has shaped a very individual way of being, something repeatedly commented on by writers and travellers. The best testimony, however, is from those who still remember, of those who begin their narrations with a, "Many years ago...". Their accounts speak of tales of rescues and the fantastic chronicles that the *Americanos* gave when they returned from overseas. They speak of a time in which the women walked around carrying the pitchers on their heads. They also speak of the arrival of homely comforts, starting with the running water and of the day when salty water no longer came out of the tap. And also of the first bare legs ever seen in the village, of the odd painters and the scandalous bohemians. They speak of the harshness of the land and, above all, of many tales of the sea. And they tell us all this in a unique way of speaking they have in these parts of the coast: the *salat* way of speaking (literally, *salted* speaking, a dialectal variant of Catalan characterised by the use of s in articles such as *Sa casa* instead of *La casa* (the house).

However, this would not be an accurate portrait of Cadaqués if we did not get closer to its human pulse, that of today and that of a not-so-distant past before the tourism arrived. How did people live in such a harsh place? What was life like in the farms? What was the pauper's path? How did they manage to humanise such a frugal landscape? How many wrecks are hidden beneath the water? What eccentric characters have left their mark beyond time? These and others are questions that breathe life into this collection of anecdotes or album of Cadaqués.

It is not easy to imagine a life that no longer exists. We do have the chronicles of those who featured in the past, and we also have the scenic spots that they made possible. Some of them are easy to reach and are magnificent to view. This is, therefore, or at least it aims to be, an invitation to the corners of Cadaqués experienced by its people.

LIGHT AND SILENCE: CALA NANS

In the eighties, the people of Cadaqués mobilised to stop the demolition of the Cala Nans lighthouse. Their fight was not in vain: this tiny lighthouse was restored and its photovoltaic plaques still turn on a light bulb every twenty seconds.

Everything indicates that Cala Nans was a place where they cast the fishing baskets, a trap to catch fish made of joints or wicker. A cove that closes the bay of Cadaqués towards the south with a promontory where, since 1856, the lighthouse has stood. The islets of Es Cucurucuc and Sa Sabolla outline, from the water, the entrance to the cove. From land, you can often see an impressive spectacle of views against the light. The fact is that the small lighthouse of Cala Nans is basically made of light and silence.

The southern end of the village is reached by a path, passing Es Llané and the beach of Sa Conca. After the last houses, the Quers, the coastal path begins which, in three kilometres, reaches the lighthouse. It is a wide path that narrows when it crosses the dry stone bridges. After the bridge of Sa Sabolla, a lime kiln bears witness to how they heated this calcareous rock to obtain an agglomeration: quicklime, which was later mixed with water and sand to form a highly resistant mortar. Further on from the kiln, the path branches off: here you can either go down to Cala Nans or continue up towards the lighthouse. If you take the path to the lighthouse, the views of the bay are magnificent.

LET'S GO TO SANT SEBASTIÀ!

"Let's go to Sant Sebastià", is what they have said for many years in Cadaqués every January. Sant Sebastià is a hermitage just a few kilometres from the village. On a plateau of the El Pení mountain, four hundred metres above sea level, is the sanctuary of Sant Sebastià. Its origin? An old surveillance tower. The current building dates back to the 18th century. It has a single nave and a semicircular apse, a doorway with a segmented arch and a discreet bell tower. Between one of its side walls and the mountain a small cave is hidden where, it is said, a shepherd found the image of the saint. The old house of the hermits is a neighbouring building which functions as a summer house enwrapped by a magnificent cork tree wood.

The hermitage, privately owned and closed throughout the year, is opened on the 20th of January to play host to the entire village of Cadaqués, the day of the annual gathering. It is the festival of Sant Sebastià. The locals walk up or reach the spot in 4-wheel drives to spend the day, often in the middle of a strong *Tramontana,* to laugh and to chat. They eat sea urchins *(garotes),* Catalan sausage omelettes and, in particular, they dance *patacades,* a violent dance accompanied by ironic and sarcastic comments about village life. The fact is, as well as being the patron saint of the village, as well as providing a fantastic view over the bay, Sant Sebastià is a licentious and necessary popular catharsis which has been preserved over the years and which in Cadaqués they love for what it is: a unique festival.

OVERSEAS BOATS

"Run up the sails! We are leaving Cadaqués!" While the crew moved about skilfully, the bay faded away in the distance. The destination? Marseilles, Genoa, Naples and, sometimes, Cuba. In the hold, wine and strong liquor: on returning, salt, cocoa and sometimes silk. It was the time of great seafaring and the Llarga beach of Cadaqués had the appearance of the international ports. Clippers, steamboats, merchant ships, fishing boats and barges shared the bay. On land were the skippers, sailors and fishermen.

Where we now see pleasure boats, when the *tramontana* or easterly wind blew, between 10 and 12 sailing ships would be huddled together waiting for the good weather. The clippers that covered the route from Valencia or Mallorca sometimes ended up in berth for too many days and their cargoes would go off. The crew disembarked to change oranges for oil, wine or fish... and to steal the heart of some innocent young lass. Sometimes, if the ships were overloaded, tons of oranges were dumped overboard that were collected on the shore with much rejoicing.

There is not much left of the seafaring past apart from memories. The old ships were taken to pieces and only on rare occasions can ships be seen anchored in the bay. The keen observer will ask why the stones from the sea on the beaches of Cadaqués are mixed with fragments of earthenware rounded by the effect of the water. They arrived in the holds of merchant ships returning from their crossing and which had been filled with ceramics to balance out the weight of the vessels. In their damp silence, they are a redoubt of that seafaring past.

A PAST OF SHIPWRECKS

The Llanishen was torpedoed in 1917 shortly after setting
sail from the port of Marseilles. The crew managed to reach
Portbou and Portvendres in two rowing boats. The ship
finally went aground in Caials. Three years later, it was the
French clipper Douamont which was wrecked in Cap de
Creus. In 1888 the fishermen of Cadaqués saved the 128
crew members of the Italian steamboat Archimedes in a
dangerous manoeuvre.

The fact is that shipwrecks and rescue operations have
formed part of the past of Cap de Creus since the remotest
times of the Romans. Among the vessels that lie on the
seabed at this point of the coast there are some, such as the
Culip IV, which sunk two thousand years ago. Experienced
navigators know that negotiating the cape on days of rough
sea is a dangerous manoeuvre, and not so much for the
height of the cliffs as for the orientation of the waters.
At the eastern end of the cape, the calm sea of the south
twists unexpectedly towards the north at a point of strong
currents. The north of the cape, a section that extends from
Cala Culip to Pla de Tudela, is an interesting underwater
archaeological site.

On days when the *tramontana* is strong, walking along
the rocky coastline of Cap de Creus is a good way of under-
standing what the seafarers mean when they talk of the devil's
cape. Diving fans can try out for themselves alongside the
wrecks that lie in Culip and Caials.

A SEA OF CORAL HUNTERS

Medusa was a mythical being that converted everything she saw into stone. Perseus beheaded her and, after the battle, went to the beach to wash his hands. On placing the monster's head on the sand, the dripping blood entered into contact with the water, solidifying it and creating the red coral.

Red coral is unique to the Mediterranean Sea. The coral known as bull's blood is of the best quality and is only formed in the waters of Cap de Creus. In ancient times it was highly valued as a protective charm and for its magical qualities. The Costa Brava was, for centuries, an authentic coral coastline. From Portvendres to Palamós an intensive coral hunting activity developed.

In 1800 Cadaqués attracted coral hunters from faraway lands such as Georges Kontos, who introduced the semi-autonomous diving suit to improve the hard extraction conditions. Until then, they dived holding their breath or with a wooden diving bell. When the inventor Narciso Monturiol –exiled in Cadaqués due to his Republican views– saw a coral hunter die in the waters of Cap de Creus, he decided to create an apparatus that would dignify these men's work. "Who lives beneath the water? The fish, My machine will take the shape of a fish". So Monturiol invented the submarine. In fact, the Ictíneu was the first submarine with the recognisable shape that has survived for posterity.

Today the coral is a protected species. In Cadaqués there are no coral hunters and to observe the coralline banks you have to dive very deep. The coral forms part of the past of a people that had always lived facing out to sea.

SMUGGLERS PARADISE

The solitary paths and coves of Cap de Creus have been a smuggler's paradise. Tobacco, coffee, silk, cocoa... the merchandise arrived on boats, was unloaded at night and hidden in the hideouts before being transported. If it is difficult today to imagine the movements of the smugglers, Josep Pla can help us with one of his tales.

"A keeled Mallorcan boat located ten or twelve miles east is outside the entrance of the bay of Cadaqués. The boat, which has avoided the beady eyes of the frontier guards, waits for the time to unload on the coast the cargo of tobacco it is carrying. Depending on the wind, it could negotiate Cap de Creus and anchor in Portaló, or moor in Jonquet. If a dangerous situation arises on disembarking, the goods will be hidden in the deposits and holes made expressly along different parts of the coast. If it is a good night, sailors and residents of the farms will load the packs on their backs and climb upstream, along solitary paths, until reaching the farms where the stock will be hidden. The group disperses once the work is done. Afterwards, at the appropriately considered time, the merchandise is packed in large casks and transported by cart and by road to wherever it has to go. You have to be very good at doing this. It is not easy. You must know how to take full advantage of the time, of the exact moment. It has to be done in secret. Taking a cart of goods from these farms to a train wagon at Llançà station requires a certain amount of willpower and spirit".

THE PAUPERS' ROUTE

Going from Cadaqués to Rosas along the Sa Cruïlla path was what was called for centuries, "the stigma of the paupers of Cadaqués". The women took the path. They loaded their baskets and filed off for the path that leaves the southernmost end of the village, after the Es Llané beach. A hellish winding path led them to the crest, in Sa Cruïlla. From there the steep drop to Roses awaited them. Four hours of abrupt paths to improve a scanty economy by selling fish. This route has seen thousands of tons of goods transported, above all, fish, wine and oil.

Covering the paupers' path is to understand the harshness of life before there were comforts as well as enjoying a view that, as it climbs, spreads out until taking in the entire bay of Cadaqués and the coastline of the Mar d'Avall. On the other side of the mountain the large coves of the Roses district await us.

The path leaves us in Cala Jòncols. It is well worth continuing as far as the nearby Cap Norfeu, one of the best-preserved points in this area, with a great biological richness and privileged etymology. It is said that Orpheus, the Greek hero who tamed the wild beasts with his music, on passing this point of the coast, sang such a beautiful tune that the Pyrenees came closer in order to listen. They came so close that, losing their balance, they fell into the sea, thus producing this small peninsula that since then has been called the cape of Orpheus.

DRY STONE PATHS AND SHEPHERDS' HUTS

A network of paths wind around the outskirts of Cadaqués, representing the patient work of generations who tamed a harsh terrain. It was necessary to survive, to have land that could be tilled, to have paths for moving around to and from the neighbouring villages and to make the region an inhabitable spot. And that is just what they did.

The kilometres of dry stone walls and the numerous shepherds' huts form part of the people's historical heritage. The infinite number of hours of human toil of the old wall builders –who selected flaky stones (the flat and laminated ones that cut so easily) to connect them one by one in an impeccable architectural fabric– are difficult to comprehend from a time measurement, ours, marked by the need to hurry.

Cap de Creus had been a landscape of woods that, even in medieval times, were gradually cut down. Fishing, –and later oil lamp fishing– consumed a large quantity of wood. The communal woods gradually disappeared and the rainwater eroded the earth. The vines and dry wall plots saved the area from impoverishment while at the same time the estates, terraces and paths were formed. The phylloxera of 1880, which killed all the stock, put paid to the golden age of wine production that was exported to France, Italy and overseas by ship to the America of free trade.

On foot, by mountain bike, by horse... going along the old stone paths means capturing the silence of Cadaqués before tourism and, above all, enjoying the scenery. After years of abandonment, the paths have been recovered in an ever-continuing task.

LIFE IN THE FARMS

A solitary life, a very harsh life that today no longer exists: the life in the farms. The farm of La Sala, in the southeast of the village, close to the Punta de la Figuera. The farm of En Baltre –in the photo–, just before the hermitage of Sant Sebastià. The Duran farm, close to Sant Baldiri. The Des Bufadors farm, that of En Melus, Sa Birba, En Godó, Des Rabassers... the abundance of farms in the Cadaqués district indicates their importance in the village's economy and life.

Positioned sheltered from the *tramontana,* they had vineyards and olive groves. They possessed herds of goats, a pair of oxen, a flock of domestic fowl and an orchard. The occupants went to Cadaqués every day to sell. They sold door-to-door. They transported the milk in a large recipient in the shape of watering can without the holes. The women waited for them with a jug in their hands. In spring, when the goats supplied more milk, they took homemade fresh and mature cheese. They also carried eggs, vegetables, and when it was time, kids and calves. They returned home with fish and produce from the city.

Some of the farms, very few in fact, are partially preserved. They can be reached by paths that leave Cadaqués, particularly around the hermitage of Sant Baldiri. They are the same paths that, years ago, would be taken by the houses' inhabitants to visit the doctor, go to school and to maintain a minimal social life. And also, naturally, to traffic in prohibited goods. This is because, let's face it, the isolation of the farms turned them into the perfect spot for hiding the smugglers' packages. For the farmers, it was a way of increasing an income that was usually a low one.

UNUSUAL PORTRAITS

Ramon of Hermosa, known for his total lack of desire to work. Lola Litus, the first bather of the village who rented out huts for changing in Es Llané. Lola Mercè, who sold the fish before going out to catch it. The gallery of Cadaqués' characters provide an extensive family album. Of all of them there was one who managed to project her name well beyond her small cosmos of sea. She was Lídia Noguer (aka Lidia Sabana).

Lídia was the daughter and wife of fishermen when in 1904 she put up Eugeni d'Ors, a renowned journalist and intellectual. Lídia, from the narrow world she inhabited, was captivated by her guest. When six years later she read the book by D'Ors, *La ben plantada* (The elegant one), she thought that it referred to her, thus beginning a long hilarious career that continued up to her death. Lídia, the Elegant One, mixed with Picasso, García Lorca and Salvador Dalí, who fired her creative capacity when reading D'Ors' articles and books in her own way.

Ors never replied to Lídia's letters. However, after she died, he wrote a book to the person who, according to him, was and was not the One with Her Feet on the Ground. Lídia of Cadaqués, who never tired of boasting about her literary identity, was however celebrated by Dalí because alongside her he had learnt his paranoiac pictorial method. The first hut the painter bought in Portlligat was sold to him by Lídia. Today, a square in Cadaqués is named after her.

THE PITCHER WOMEN

There was a time when there was no money in the village. You went to the spring for water. The fire was only lit if you had gone to look for wood or coal. Dirty clothes were taken in baskets to the public washhouse. Food was obtained from the orchard. Soap was made manually in the street... and a long list of other activities undertaken to cover the basic necessities.

In Cadaqués, as in other villages in this country, a great deal of this work was the responsibility of the womenfolk. What was a particular trait of this coastal spot was the way of carrying the goods; baskets, boxes, packets... or pitchers, everything was carried on their head: an ingenious system that frees the hands and keeps the body firm. One of the most well-known icons of Cadaqués, recreated by Dalí and other painters, is that showing an elegant woman with the pitcher on her head. This image forms part of the people's memory and emphasises what has been repeated over an over again: the influence of women in the village's past.

In Cadaqués, the *sardanas* were danced by the women, who sang wholeheartedly while they danced. In Cadaqués, the woman's surname was used for the children's surnames and, quite often, the husband's too. In Cadaqués legends grew about women with witches' powers: women who cast spells on the boats so that they would return with empty nets. What was the secret to all this? The answer is easy: when the fishing kept the men busy for weeks on end –and this was not exclusive to Cadaqués– the community remained, inevitably, in the hands of the women.

SERVICES AND INFORMATION OF INTERÉST

SPORTS

Cadaqués and its environs allow you undertake numerous sporting activities, especially those related to the sea such as deep-sea diving, and also provide unusual routes along the old stone paths of Cap de Creus. The seabed of this coast conceals archaeological treasures and an interesting variety of flora and fauna.

▶ DIVING

Diving Center Cadaqués. Sa Conca 972 25 90 36
Es Caials. Es Caials, s/n 676 44 38 69
Scuba World. C. Font Vella, 5 629 4 13 80
Sotamar Diving Center.
Av. Caritat Serinyana, 17 972 25 88 76
Tauchbasis Ulla + Paul.
Punta de s'Oliguera, s/n 972 25 89 80
Up Down. Riba Pianc, s/n 609 21 33 29

▶ KAYAK

Kayak Portlligat. Platja de Portlligat 639 97 93 89

▶ HORSE RIDING

Centre Hípic Cadaqués.
Paratge Mas Duran, s/n 972 19 90 12

▶ TREKKING

Gorgònia. *Servei de Guies* 669 826 321
Guides to the Natural Park of Cap de Creus.
Itineraries, guided visits and VTT routes
Espai Cap de Creus/
Cap de Creus Lighthouse 972 25 83 15
Monastery of Sant Pere de Rodes/Palau de l'Abat
Information Centre 972 19 31 91

▶ MARITIME ROUTES

Cruceros Cadaqués. 972 15 94 62
Ones. *Kayak, sailing, etc.* Platja Gran 686 79 91 94

▶ SPORTS CENTRES
Polisportiu Municipal.
Cra. Cap de Creus, s/n 972 25 86 07

FESTIVALS AND TRADITIONS

In love with their past and their customs, in Cadaqués they have preserved the everlasting festivals and traditions. Some, like the festival of Sant Sebastià, are hundreds of years old. Others, like the International Music Festival, held since the nineteen-seventies, attract a cosmopolitan audience. In Cadaqués there are festivals throughout the year to satisfy all tastes.

▶ **L'aplec del Sol Ixent a Cap de Creus (The Festival of the Rising Sun in Cap de Creus).** At 7 o'clock in the morning on January the 1st the new day's light is welcomed in from the esplanade of the lighthouse with cake and chocolate. It is a good idea to get there early because more and more people gather there each year.

▶ **L'aplec de Sant Sebastià (Festival of Sant Sebastià).** On the 20th of January of each year a trip is made to the hermitage of Sant Sebastià. On the side facing the Pení mountain they dance and sing *patacades* and eat sea urchins.

▶ **El carnaval (Carnival).** Every Ash Wednesday the people licentiously take to the streets for three days. If the carnival in Roses is one of the most spectacular in the region, the one at Cadaqués is known for its over-the-top behaviour!

▶ **La Cuina de ses Dones (The women's cuisine).**
During the second fortnight of April, within the Cultural Week, a gastronomic show is held of local cuisine prepared by the women of the village.

▶ **La processó del Carme (The procession of Carmen).** 16th of July, the patron saint of seafarers. The figure of the virgin is carried on the sailors' shoulders and boards a fishing boat which is followed by an entourage of adorned boats.

▶ **Internacional Music Festival of Cadaqués.** Since the nineteen-seventies a pioneering festival has been held every August on the Costa Brava that brings together the very best of international classical music.

▶ **Festa Major d'estiu (Summer Annual Festival).** 11th of September. Among the other activities a lateen sail meeting and rowing boat regatta are held.

▶ **Festa Major d'hivern (Winter Annual festival).** 18th of December

MUSEUMS AND ART GALLERIES

The connection between Cadaqués and art began when the selfsame 20th century dawned. Strolling around the village streets provides you with the chance to enjoy the delights of numerous galleries and art studios. As well as the well-known Salavador Dalí House-Museum in Portlligat, Cadaqués has a Municipal Art Museum, which every year organises monographic exhibitions of artists with a connection to the village, and with the Casino exhibition rooms, an unbeatable and recently restored setting facing the sea.

▶ **MUSEUMS**
Salvador Dalí House-Museum. *Visits every 10 minutes. By prior arrangement only.*
Portlligat, s/n   972 25 10 15
Espai Cap de Creus.
Cap de Creus Lighthouse   972 25 83 15
Museu de Cadaqués. C. Monturiol, 15   972 25 88 77
Sala l'Amistat. Plaça Dr. Trèmols, 1   972 25 88 00

▶ **ART GALLERIES**
Àmbit Artístic. C. Horta d'en Sanés, 9   654 42 47 72
Cadaqués Dos. C. Horta d'en Sanés, 7   972 25 91 55
Galeria de la Riba. Riba Pianc, 2   972 25 90 26
Galeria l'Amistat. Plaça Dr. Trèmols, 1 972 25 88 00
Marges-U. C. Unió, 12   972 25 85 43
                                                        972 25 87 03
Portdoguer. C. Guillem Bruguera, s/n
Portlligat. Av. Salvador Dalí, 1   972 25 81 62

▶ **GALLERIES-STUDIOS**
Cadaqués Art Studio. C. Dr. Callís, 20   972 25 91 16
Lionel Neguiral. C. Dr. Callís, 18   972 25 91 16
Taller Galeria Fort.
C. Horta d'en Sanés, 9-11   972 25 85 49

WHERE TO EAT

Fresh fish and seafood cuisine that has the most magnificent ingredients: as many as 150 species of fish, local market garden produce and an excellent olive oil: and all served with local wines, which have been awarded the D.O. label for years now: Empordà-Costa Brava. The gastronomic offer of Cadaqués covers all budgets.

Casa Anita. C. Miquel Rosset, 16 972 25 84 71
Grilled fish in the context of a bohemian atmosphere.
Cala Bona. Cra. Portlligat, s/n 972 25 85 37
Rice with crabmeat.
Can Rafa. Passeig de Mar, 7 972 15 94 01
Suquet (fish stew) and lobster from Cap de Creus.
Cap de Creus. Cap de Creus, s/n 972 19 90 05
Fresh fish and Indian cuisine. Magnificent views
and unique atmosphere.
Casa Nun. Portitxó, 6 972 25 88 56
Fresh fish, modern cuisine and homemade desserts
in a very well thought out setting.
El Barroco. C. Nou, s/n 972 25 86 32
Oriental dishes, vegetarian cuisine and Catalan
specialities such as squid filled with ratatouille.
Es Trull. Portitxó, 5 972 15 93 32
Fish from Cap de Creus.
La Galiota. C. Monturiol, 9 972 25 81 87
Sea bass with fennel, marinated salmon.
Sa Gambina. Riba Nemesi Llorens, s/n 972 25 81 27
Rice dishes and casseroles.
Vehí. C. Església, 6 972 25 84 70
Freshly caught fish in a homely atmosphere.

▶ *And also at:*
Al Gianni. Riera Sant Vicens, s/n 972 25 83 71
Can Pelayo. C. Pruna, 11 972 25 83 56
Can Tito. C. Vigilant, s/n 972 25 90 70
Casa dels Pernils. C. Miquel Rosset, 7 972 25 85 24
Casa Pilar. C. Miranda, 4 972 25 87 01
Chez Pierre. C. Miquel Rosset, 48 972 25 84 16
Don Quijote. Av. Caritat Serinyana, s/n 972 25 81 41
El Pescador. Riba Nemesi Llorens, s/n 972 25 88 59
El Tibèric. C. Curós, s/n 600 07 58 98
Es Balconet. C. Sant Antoni, 2 972 25 88 14

Es Baluart. Riba Nemesi Llorens, 2 972 25 81 83
Es Racó. C. Dr. Callís, 3 972 15 94 80
Horta d'en Rahola.
Paratge Tarongeta, s/n 972 25 10 49
Ix. C. Horta d'en Sanés, 1 972 25 87 33
La Cala. Av. Caritat Serinyana, 4 972 25 85 04
La Font. C. Miquel Rosset, 6 972 25 88 57
La Sirena. C. Call, s/n 972 25 89 74
Pizzeria César. C. Curós, 11 972 25 88 06
Pizzeria El Boliche.
C. Miquel Rosset, s/n
Pizzeria La Gritta. Passeig, 11 972 15 94 71
Pizzeria Plaza. Passeig, 10 972 15 94 74
S'Entina. Plaça Dr. Trèmols, 6 972 25 80 61
Sa Grota. C. Nou, 11 972 25 83 80
Sol Ixent. Es Caials, s/n 972 25 89 02
Spagheteria La Lluna.
C. Miquel Rosset, s/n 972 25 85 96
Suarri. C. Vigilant, 3 972 25 91 28
Tiramisú. C. Miquel Rosset, 8 972 25 81 33

WHERE TO STAY
▶ **HOTELS**
Llané Petit ***
C. Doctor Bartomeus, 37 972 25 10 20
Octavia *** Riera Sant Vicens, s/n 972 15 92 25
Playa Sol *** Platja Pianc, 3 972 25 81 00
Rocamar *** Rocamar, s/n 972 25 81 50
Sa Guarda *** Cra. Portlligat, 28 972 25 80 82
Blaumar ** C. Massa d'Or, 21 972 15 90 20
La Tarongeta ** C. Sant Vicens, s/n 972 25 82 89
La Residència ** Av. C. Serinyana, 1 972 25 83 12
Misty ** Cra. nova de Portlligat, s/n 972 25 89 62
Nou Estrelles ** C. Sant Vicens, s/n 972 25 91 00

Portlligat ** Platja Portlligat, s/n 972 25 81 62
Cap de Creus * Cap de Creus, s/n 972 19 90 05
Ubaldo * C. Unió, 13 972 25 81 25

▶ **GUEST HOUSES**
Casa Europa ** Paratge Maltret, s/n 972 25 81 31
Hostal Cristina ** Riera, 1 972 25 81 38
Hostal El Ranxo **
Av. Caritat Serinyana, s/n 972 25 80 05
Hostal Marina ** Riera, 3 972 15 90 91
Fonda Cala d'Or * C. Tórtora, 2 972 25 81 49
Fonda Vehí * C. Església, 6 972 25 84 70
La Fonda * C. Tórtora, 64 972 25 80 19

▶ **RESIDENCIES AND APARTAMENTS**
Carpe Diem Club. *Apartaments*
Cra. Cap de Creus, s/n 972 25 81 31
Residència Calina. *Apart-hotel*
Platja Portlligat, s/n 972 25 88 51

▶ **ESTATE AGENCIES**
Agència I. Cadaqués. Passeig, 6 972 25 82 66
Agència Pianc. Pianc, 9 972 25 80 06
Agència Serintec.
Av. Caritat Serinyana, 8 972 25 85 92
Agència Soms-Granados.
Av. Caritat Serinyana, 20 972 25 10 06
Agència Tibau. C. Miquel Rosset, 2 972 25 10 27

▶ **CAMP SITES**
Cadaqués (2ª). Crta. Portlligat, 17 972 25 81 26

▶ **PUBLIC TRANSPORT**
SARFA. C. Sant Vicens, s/n 972 25 87 13
Coach route
Cadaqués/Roses/Figueres/Girona/Barcelona

▶ **TAXIS**
Josep Giró. Av. Caritat Serinyana, 23 972 25 87 71
Olé Taxi. 626 52 68 32

▶ **BOAT HIRE**
Bikes & Boats Cadaqués.
Platja des Poal, s/n 972 25 80 27
Motonàutica Almarc.
Pla del Sr. Llorens, s/n 972 25 84 17
Motonàutica Llonch.
Av. Caritat Serinyana, s/n 972 25 83 53
Motonàutica Manel.
Av. Caritat Serinyana, s/n 972 15 91 35
Motonàutica Vinyes. Cra. Roses, s/n 972 25 80 69
Nàutica Cala Nans.
Pla del Sr. Llorens, s/n 659 99 34 56
Nàutica R. Morales.
Pla del Sr. Llorens, s/n 626 42 99 63

▶ **BOAT HIRE / CRUISES**
Barca Gala. Platja de Portlligat, s/n 607 26 57 85
Creuers Cadaqués. 972 15 94 62
Sant Isidre. *Classic vessel* 972 25 80 27

▶ **MOUNTAIN BIKE AND MOPED HIRE**
Bikes & Boats. Platja des Poal, s/n 972 25 80 27
Rent @ Bit. Av. Caritat Serinyana, 9 972 25 10 23

▶ **PETROL STATION** *Open: 8 a.m. to 9 p.m.*
Av. Caritat Serinyana, s/n 972 25 81 89

PUBLIC SERVICES AND ORGANISATIONS

Town Hall. C. Silvi Rahola, 2   972 25 82 00
Tourism Office.
Open: 10 a.m. to 1 p.m. and 4 to 8 p.m.
Sundays and public holidays: 10 a.m. to 1 p.m.
Winter: closed on Sundays and public holidays.
C. Cotxe, 2 - A   972 25 83 15
Post office. *Open: 9 a.m. to 2 p.m.*
Saturday: 9 a.m. to 1 p.m.
C. Rierassa, 11   972 25 87 98
Natural Park of Cap de Creus Office.
Espai Cap de Creus/
Cap de Creus Lighthouse   972 25 83 15
Monastery of Sant Pere de Rodes/Palau de l'Abat
Information Centre   972 19 31 91
Ràdio Cap de Creus 88'8 FM.
C. Carles Rahola, 9   972 15 92 00
Weekly market. *Mondays. Venue:* Riera Sant Vicens
Medical assistance. C. Nou, 6   972 25 88 07

▶ EMERGENCIES

Fire. C. Carles Rahola, 11   972 25 80 08
Mossos d'Esquadra (Catalan Police).
Cra. Les Arenes, s/n. Roses   972 15 27 77
Urgències   088
Local Police. C. Carles Rahola, 9   972 15 93 43
Red Cross.   972 20 04 15
Maritime Emergencies.   900 20 2202

▶ CHEMISTS

F. Moradell. Plaça Frederic Rahola, 19   972 25 87 51
F. Colomer. Cra. Portlligat, s/n   972 25 89 32

WEBSITES

www.costabrava.org *Culture, accommodation, gastronomy... miscellaneous info about Cadaqués and the Costa Brava.*
www.gihostaleria.org *Web of the Hoteliers Federation of the Girona Counties.*
www.dali-estate.org *Web of the Fundación Gala-Salvador Dalí. Information about the House –Museum of Portlligat (visits, opening times...).*
http://altemporda.ddgi.es *Routes, info, services... about Cadaqués. Full and updated information from the Girona Provincial Council.*
www.turismegirona.com *All the info and services that may be useful.*
www.acadaques.com *Very complete search engine about Cadaqués: you will find everything or nearly everything.*
www.cbrava.com *Electronic newspaper "Cap de Creus online". Updated daily: weather, the state of the sea and latest news.*
http://geo.ya.com/cadaques2001 *Collection of stories from Cadaqués, stories about life and historical news told by the local Cadaqués people. Very curious.*
http://pieraedicions.com/cadaques *Map, photos, routes and itineraries from Cadaqués.*
www.publintur.es/guiacata/cbrava/cadaques *Guide to the towns of the Costa Brava. Updated information.*

© 2004 **Triangle Postals SL**

Concept Jordi Puig

© **Photography** Jordi Puig
pages 91, 110-111, 112, 113, 115, 116, 117, 118, 119, 120-121,
122, 123, 124, 125 © JordiPuig / Fundació Gala- Salvador Dalí, 2004
pages 64-65, 66 © Pere Vivas / Jordi Puig
pages 140, 141, 173 © Arnald Plujá.
page 171 © Miquel Pontes.
page 183 Eugeni d'Ors archive/ Arxiu Nacional de Catalunya.
page 185 Antoni Planells, photograph by permission of Cadaqués Town Council.
page 27 © Salvador Dalí, Fundació Gala- Salvador Dalí, VEGAP, Figueres, 2004.

© **Text** Cristina Masanés

© **Translation** Steve Cedar

© **Ilustrations** Perico Pastor

Graphic design Sabina Monza

Photomechanics Tecnoart
Printed by NG Nivell Gràfic   07/2006

Reg. number B-33.612.2004
ISBN 84-8478-139-9

Triangle Postals SL
Sant Lluís, Menorca
tel +34 971 15 04 51
fax +34 971 15 18 36
triangle@infotelecom.es
www.trianglepostals.com